Red Riding Hood's Dilemma

for my family

March 2011

RED RIDING HOOD'S DILEMMA

For Maureen + Benno

Good to have met you +
Thank you

Órfhlaith Foyle

**ARLEN
HOUSE**

Red Riding Hood's Dilemma

is published in 2010 by
ARLEN HOUSE
an imprint of Arlen Publications Ltd
PO Box 222
Galway
Ireland
Phone/Fax: 353 86 8207617
Email: arlenhouse@gmail.com
www.arlenhouse.ie

International distribution:
SYRACUSE UNIVERSITY PRESS
621 Skytop Road, Suite 110
Syracuse, New York
USA 13244–5290
Phone: 315–443–5534/Fax: 315–443–5545
Email: supress@syr.edu
www.syracuseuniversitypress.syr.edu

ISBN 978–0–905223–64–3
(a signed and numbered limited edition is also available)

Typesetting ¦ Arlen House
Printing ¦ Brunswick Press
Cover Artwork ¦ Pauline Bewick

CONTENTS

RED RIDING HOOD'S DILEMMA

Should I kill the wolf
or invite him to tea?
Sit him down with a
napkin draped upon his lap
and feed him sponge fingers
instead of me?

PUSS IN BOOTS

I have boots with the ears of a cat,
a toe size too big for me
with wide zip lips
that growl and possibly purr.
Skin of dark wine
and a spine - up the back
crinkled rolls of leathered fur,
where my paws fit in.
The length of my leg
- notch at my ankle bone
A devil's knuckle flexed out of sight
- viewed in this light

nothing is sinuous
- nothing with a darkened nightmare tint.
Nothing I can - hint.
If I could - and preferably I would
- I would mask it all.

The sleek slip of velvet fur underneath
where my bones ripple then sigh when you touch.
How easy it would be
- not to risk.
Just to be - smooth, glass-shiny with a smile
calibrated to catch you in any pub crawl.

But if I did
- if I suited up into proper skin
of the kind you are in
- if I did that ...
then you would not get
- my kind of cat.

THERE IS A PAINTING I KNOW

'The Night Café' by Vincent van Gogh.

There is a painting I know
with a mad slithering light
and it succours every crazed eye.
In it
desperate lovers
kiss.
Isolated drinkers
drink.
And the painter,
his lips to my shoulder,
says merely
This is a slice of Damnation.

PHOTOGRAPH OF HER BROTHER'S SKULL

They give you to me,
a numbered skull from a high shelf
and in my hand you are
a strange brute thing – a thing I hardly see
– my brother.

The clean smooth bone of you
– the whole of you no longer with me.
In this room of discovered skulls,
I have lost my memories
and the photographer fixes your dead stare
for his lens.

In this room of skulls
your face is lost,
my brother,
and I grip hard to what is left.

THE MAN FROM THE SECOND WORLD WAR

The man from the Second World War
came into our sweet shop today.
He stood by the Fry's Chocolate glass mirror
and smoked all his cares away.
He had old man's hands and old man's eyes
and his clothes smelled of sweat and piss.
He was too old to be friendly to
and too dried up to kiss.

As we sometimes did - for old people who asked.
A kiss for those - who my grandmother said
- were sometimes better off dead.

She was used to his kind
- men who screamed like children inside
and the man from the Second World War
had something to hide.
He once flew spitfires straight into German skies,
and we - buoyed up with cartoon and childish thrill
asked him
- 'what's it like to really kill?'

DAMN THEM

Damn the purists
and their love of rightness.
their pure fear of love.

Give me life.
Give me Gods.
Give me flesh.

Damn pristine elite-ness
of manner,
cool, well-toned voices
cautious and serene.
Damn manufactured spirits
of beauty
of careful love
of controlled lives.

Give me wide, wild spirits.
Give me terrible, tumbling passion.
Give me love
that rips my soul
open to you.
Give me the lust of your eyes
that slams against my body.
Give me your wetness,
your skin.

I damn their hateful saintliness,
their rules of normality.
they watch us with snake-like caution.

We love
you and I
and damn them.

JESUS IN THE PAINTING, MARY IN BLUE

When I was a young girl, prayers had magic words.
Holy Mary,
Hail Mary.
Make me good.
Even Jesus guaranteed it.
On the top of the stairs of my grandparents' house,
He laid his breast open as I went to bed.
Yet the nuns ignored my invisible sins through their black
and white masks.
And the priests erased my confessions with Day-Glo
blessings.
Jesus in the Painting
Mary in Blue.

I did not turn out good.
I wrote instead
and I used words with their goodness turned inside out.
Like the dark inside of Jesus' breast
is the dark inside of anyone's breast.
You in the Painting
Me in Blue.

An uncle condemned me
– *you invite the devil to sit down beside you*
but you are Jesus in the Painting
and I am Mary in Blue.
Lay your breast open
right to the warm meat of your heart,
and the magic prayers of the past
must now lay down their man-made gold.
Because it is:
You in the Painting and
Me in Blue.

BUSH WIFE

Once she was reduced to begging.
Slipping to her knees, her mouth
at his ear.
This is your conscience speaking.
And she magicked a desperate smile.
Bring me back something sweet,
something kind,
or chocolate.
But he left as usual,
thirty miles into the bush towards town,
thought of her only as a remnant,
something to pick up when he got back.
Pick up and twist
when she was useful again.
By the way, he mentioned once,
three men died in the hole we dug today.
He looked at her as he ate:
Funny. Life is cheap here.

First Love Song of 2006

If you were to see me,
really see me.
I would be someone
I could not recognise.
It's a truth I cannot redress.
But I am a mess.
An odd rhyme
– undone
– split into threads
– sinewed onto bone.
My swim of guts
barely seem my own.

And so you see.
The smile is a little stretched
because even I can't see behind it.
Perhaps it wouldn't fit
– if you imagine I am as gentle
as I play,
or as soft as I say
– 'I love you. All my selves love you'.
And I watch you
for all your hidden selves

And I pray
– that there is such a thing as an
honest duel of two.

THESE THINGS EXHILARATE MY SOUL

These things exhilarate my soul:
Bark underfoot.
A vast wind's terrifying brilliance.
An uncurled sun at night.
And you. Just you.

THE KILLERS' CHANT

It is easy to see what killers we are.
And the animal bones that encase our heart.
And the drip, drip
blood on our tongue
keeps us fed.

It is easy to see what liars we are.
Dancing with made-up smiles in our mouths.
And the beat, beat
hate in our eyes
keeps us heard.

It is easy to see what poisoners we are.
Medieval goosesteps in our boots.
And the blast, blast
death in our hands
keeps us alive.

It is easy to see who our enemies are.
On a chessboard of mathematical moves,
they keep us checked.
It is easy to see the dead between us,
roll into their graves.

And the reasons, the reasons
grow heads of snakes and feet of clay
forever ... and a day.

THE STRANGER

To grow in one place.
To root your feet and say
'I am of this place.
The skin of this people's skin is mine.
Their talk, my talk.
Their smell is mine'.
You prefer the stranger to remain lost.
His talk could unleash witches' spells
so you don't listen to his story.
Yet you watch his skin and in pubs,
in houses like your own,
you talk about the stranger,
relieved he is not you

LOVE PROMISE

Love delivers as promised:
Make me into a lie
and I will defeat you.
Make me into a truth
and I will destroy you.
Make me into your lover
and I will invade you.
Make me into your child
and I will negate you.

Love seeks qualification:
So tell me
– why do you then make me your food?

Love is answered:
Let us talk about the strange cliché of the heart.
It adds one life to another.
It absolves the lie.
It creates truth.
And negation is anyone's beginning.

DESPITE EVERYTHING

Despite everything.
Despite it all.
This comes ...
with the late day's
evening breath.
Where are you to feel all this?

Boy Reading Book

Maybe his mother had never realised
how the boy understood the curious truth
of Bunny Suicides.
Even I had not read the book.
But the boy read it.
I watched his eyes behind his glasses and he may have
been six years old.
But to know that suicide in the bunny world was not only
endemic but comedic
was a precisely adult thing in a boy
and it made him laugh.

The comic his mother had given him
was still in his right hand
but the suicidal bunnies were in his left.
I wondered if they had cut their own throats or perhaps
boiled themselves,
dead of whatever pain they could not escape.
All done in cartoon fun.

So I half-understood when his mother confiscated the
book after she had returned with her coffee and his juice.
But he had been laughing too much at the pictures
and once at me when he saw me smile at him,

because I seemed to appreciate
that even bunnies can do human things
that we don't ever want to see.

REVENGE

You had forgotten my
wolf-like tendencies.
Once your laugh had
shamed my anxious lips.
I amused your eyes.
My love was nothing.

So I made you shiver.
I told you how
I longed to purge you
of what you truly
loved
– an appreciation of revered
tackiness.
The sort you see on
popular catwalks.

I reminded you.
Your hands skittered
at your breast.
I dredged up passionate words.
Your eyes stopped on my face.
My words smothered your little
mundane heart.
Squeaked it clean.
I pleasured my soul.
I watched you dwindle.

Someone should have
warned you what
love can do.

FIRE

I could suppose that you do not exist.
I could suppose that you are nothing but a
collection of magic and the dark stories of
hunters who saw fire for the first time.

I want to be such a hunter.
To smell my own cooling sweat of fear
and draw a face in the smoke,
then hear your voice in the stones
and lie beneath the whole eye of sky.

How convenient it is to thread you
from the earth and heaven;
from the inside of a woman and
from the sky whose arms reach down
to pluck you
out.

And if you are the jigsaw of Tacitus's memory
and recycled legends
does that make me less real
in all my fear and joy?

I could suppose that the planets turn
on your fingers and your spit
once sewed up
Adam's joints,
and your breath lined his lungs
as you are meant to have done mine.

Or I could suppose that I am lost somewhere
between the genetic uselessness of
your existence and my gut-deep
animal need for your hands
to be inside mountains.

I could insist that you are not worthy of a capital 'You'.
I could ignore Blake and those angels of his
when I see a flower,
and marvel instead at the precision of
stamen and petal.

I could ignore St Teresa under Bernini's hand,
the shadow of her flesh in stone
– or the dark voiceless breathing in the
high painted vaults of churches where
others came and went in their own lives
beading prayers to wishes.

Or I could suppose instead
that you exist because
those who only see
worm food inside us
don't understand what the hunters saw,
when their fire-magic lifted the stars
and gave them a god
to fill in the emptiness of death.

GROWL

Dark water groin of lake,
the rooted grass-yellow skin of mountains,
the body of me
is laid out in these things
and against you.
So when or if the mountain cracks
and the lake opens its mouth
with its liquid tongue
in a slurp of beauty,
and the Pied Piper whistles from a
crevasse,
I would have to think twice about
following you and him
to a place where all things are good
and finish the same,
and nothing is queer, or strange,
or conscious of how Evil wears its truth
inside out,
or how love is coated by death
that even the heart has no advantage.
And where 'Happy Ever After'
is a prayer civilised enough
to withstand every dark growl
of my skin against yours.

And immediately you are old in your comfort.
Since the Pied Piper has brought you your slippers
and the rats have disappeared,
except for me ...
I hold my fingers to frame the lake,
I don't listen to your words, and
in the evening I will tell someone of
where I left you, and I will try not to
see it as a failure
that I lost you.

DANCE

Imagine me in a man's arms
the buttons of my dress pressed into his shirt.
Music and evening sun
the kind of heat that gives sheen to everyone's skin.
I taste my man's sweat as I kiss his chest where
his shirt is unbuttoned to his breast-bone.
I lay my forehead where I've kissed him.
I can smell us both.
Feel his lips in my hair.
This life.
This need to seep into love and not only him
but what is around us.
The laughing, drunk sixty-year-old woman in the corner,
low slung orange dress and puckered breast,
red lips reciting poetry she composed yesterday to a young
male. A student of her life.
He wants her thirst for life.
My lover holds my waist.
Our hip-bones find anchor in each other.
Old men's eyes gleam.
They smoke cigars and drink local brandy.
They watch us dance and sing.
Their own voices add to the slow gut-drive of a lone
trumpet. It is good to be who I am in my lover's arms.
I think of our bed and the stone floor.
Shutters – never curtains.
The bristling, hot human night outside.
My love, I call him.
My love.

MISSED OPPORTUNITY

One evening I walked
with someone I nearly knew.
He spoke of Alaska and cabin fever,
trees in Ashland, Oregon
LSD and apparitions of
God.
Of course I was already in love
with someone else,
not too different
and reasonably safe.

IF I COULD

If I could
I'd pray for your resurrection
after four years
when I screamed inside
and remembered I must have loved you.
Instead, I am faced with other things:
The last drunken night and
that other body that smelled
too sour and too real.

AFTER SUNDAY MASS IN MALAWI

After Sunday Mass they whispered:
'He was a poet perhaps.
A dissident, yes.
He ignored the spies in his classroom'.
Then someone else also remembered:
'Of course, this is not our country.
We are Whites, you see,
and cannot disappear so easily'.

And Where Else?

Sometimes we were mistaken for Canadians
and because we replied Australian,
we seemed to make sense.
School friends demanded why we weren't black
since we came from Africa too.
And where else?
Well, we climbed the ant-hills on the way to Mombasa.
Spoke Swahili but lived on Kikuyu land.
We avoided the secret police in Malawi,
grew used to the prison fence that hid
'The Disappeared',
and in Australia, we learned
Irish are preferred to English,
Greeks and Italians are nicknamed 'Wogs'
and Aboriginals must look good for the tourists.
And where else?
There's Russia and Lenin's corpse,
Israel, bombs in the market place and
Turkish delight under our pillows.
And where else?
And it was easy to explain away.
Well ... you see, we'd say
our parents are Irish
but really,
we're from somewhere else.

ITALIAN NUNS

In Kenya, we knew Italian nuns
who snapped chicken necks
and swung pig sausage from the
kitchen rafters.
They smelled of soup and incense
and dug their fingers into our cheeks
– a sign of endearment.
Dangerous women, we decided
and loved them back.
We dragged dead pigeons to their door
and walked barefoot in their rooms.
Sometimes they seemed to pray,
but when they called to the chickens,
my sister, brother and I
sat, watched and waited.

RELIGIOUS THOUGHTS

Is God all love? All force. Life force.
Is love a force? We are loved
and fed well with this force,
yet if we distil it, use it
for convenience,
may it not be evil?
and if so, if we cause evil
may it not reverberate against us?
so God ... loves us. Is us.
But if we misuse
does not our love pervert us?

SOMEONE CREPT UP TO ME

Someone crept up to me
knowledgeable and sweet, with
an eye for my sins.
They spoke of belief.
They spoke of love.
They kept me close and
prepared me a Bible.
Open pages of logical verse.
Sin and counter-sin.
Of blood revenge and life
reined in with rules
that deemed me lost yet
branded me a recoverable
whore.
Their army, I was assured, possessed
God's Heart.
Their war and their will had
His Mark.
But I spat out their goodness
like spare vomit from my lungs.
I developed my own blasphemy.
I prefer my love with its own mind.
I prefer my belief with its own heart.

ANTHEM FOR THE DUMB

Who wouldn't like to be dumb?
To be loved up with TV-sponsored thoughts
and wait for the delivery to come
– mailed to your door.
And men with teeth-shining promises of
we can give you more!

Who wouldn't want to be dumb?
To witness your life as far as
your eye can see,
and what is 'outside'
is never a 'me'.

And those whose faces don't
match yours
are in reality – bores
with their shredded, dark lives
dirtying up your floors.

So who wouldn't love to be dumb?
who wouldn't love to *Get Me Some!*
of plasticated, press out and assembled lives
where thinking only ever matters
if it only ever lies.

ACCORDING TO ALBERT SPEER

According to Albert Speer – it did Hitler good to speak
of his dreams.
Of his Volkshalle and the river of blond hair of its people.
His people – sufficiently bleached to suit the new avenues.
No Jews. Or those others deficient in some other way.
They are tidied away in crematorium squares – in Polish
woods and sub-Siberian camps.
While in Hitler's dreams his Triumph arch is the mark of
his Europe and its image keeps the devils away.

According to Albert, Hitler needed his dreams to soothe
his hands; although spotless white – they had fashioned
death – into well-made plans that fitted amongst the
laughter and cigarette smoke of men with heavy smiles
convinced that the Yellow Star was the perfect totem of
sensible erasure.

And in the future when Hitler's Toy Town is placed in
exact replica scale – pure white in a large room – with a
quiet audience and history creeping on the sidelines
– some will say the unthinkable – how beautiful the dream
was and then you must glance at the room's corners and
wonder what hides there, as it hides there in people's
minds.

How Berlin reinvented in Hitler's dreams
possessed none of history's squalor,
but had the ruled efficiency of a Thousand Year Reich
and how long ago it all was.
And how nothing like this will ever happen again.
Which is as convenient a lie as Albert ever used
and as Hitler understood,
when they sat and talked and built their dream
from another people's bones.

WORDS SAID TO A POET JUST BEFORE HER/HIS DEMISE

Poetry is useless.
It only uses words and
they can be rubbed out.
Same way as we
rub you out.
Blank.
You're gone.
Just a vacancy,
not even a breath left.
But
– if you insist
to exist – in books
well ... then ...
we can burn you up ...
all over again.

AKHMATOVA

My words cannot delineate you
as Modigliani drew
from the dark Paris mornings
and later during the 'Terror',
you wandered mad at
the edge.
Three lovers gone.
A son imprisoned.
Perhaps the death-choked
eyes of Tsvetaeva
haunted you.
Beloved exiles beckoned.
But you,
you turned your body,
tall, inviolate
and breathed
blood-fingered air.

TO THE GIRL BUYING *WUTHERING HEIGHTS*

You are fourteen years old
and I want to be you again.
Emily is calling
and Heathcliff has tethered the horses.
Your hair is like mine
and I can predict how your
heart will beat
like so ... because of Emily's words,
and the dark heath and wind
like a man's hand touching you.
Where ... you do not know.
But you feel it
between your lungs
and you see it
in the dark slide of the sun
against the earth.

QUINCE FLOWERS

Quince flowers weave the daffodils into their spell.
Speak to her, they order.
Remind her of her future.
The earth has

– it has sucked on the
woman's fleshed bones.
It has implored the wind to call her.
The wind curls at her ears,
swoons at her throat.
It lies against her trembling
heart – sodden with a
terrifying promise:

Allow me to end your life.
I will bleach your soul empty.
I will adorn you with bird song.
Earth's blood will crawl your
veins open to her kiss.
Death – a knowing beauty – will
press your dying lips.
Her breath will rot you of educated fantasies.
They litter your feet.
Do not touch!
Grant me you demise.
I shall melt your flesh.
Dance your disassembled bones anew
into a new breathing.

The woman reaching
– allows the quince to
bracelet her wrist.

The Daemon

You come alive as I rest.
To ponder my careful guidelines.
You rise shining from me.
You are lean.
Stalking my normal air.
You want my life riddled with you.
My eyes to speak of your demon beauty.
My hands to shape your desires.
You glide derisively within my learned beliefs.
You snarl at my timidity.
So ...
you enter my dreams.
Your eyes fill mine.
I breathe you hard.
I feel your smile curve.
I feel you.
But ...
when I am awake, you are gone – repelled.
Sliding into the seams of my skin,
to prowl my hidden heart.
I keep you there.
Veiled.
Breathing only through my pen.

I COME FROM

I come from
dark red concrete floors,
hands in the dark on doors.
I come from
men and women carved
into silent conversation.
I come from
hot wide grass where
animals kill.
I come from
reading books in my room.
I come from
watching a dictator speak to
schoolchildren while
I sat in a tree.
I come from priests who
visited
in the afternoons
with the best cake on show.
I come from an English accent
and the White fear of the Black.
I come from the fear of God also
and my mother's tears
and my father's sharp dreams
buried down
into mine and
mixed with words
that would like to
Burn – It – All – Down
– Sometime.

ROMANCE WITH PARIS

Toulouse is missing
and I can't stand Paris.
The measly smiles
from the sex workers,
nor the Eiffel Tower's
'Bling Bling'.
Hemingway has disappeared
and Josephine Baker
isn't dancing anymore.

And I'm too young
not to notice the
urined streets
and the resined faces
of the street kids
on the Boulevard de Clichy,
side-stepping Metro vents
and finishing deals.

Since Toulouse is always missing
and Monmartre is a backstreet
and the Moulin Rouge
flounces its doors
– I should be picking up
stories from the stones.
Instead I buy a Nutella crepe
from the hands of
a Congolese girl.

C'est bon? I say.
C'est bon, she shrugs.

And like van Gogh,
The night above dives
bright into darkness

while bodies peel
from walls – and a boy
touches me
but I don't touch back.
Instead – I eat my chocolate mess
and so damn my frail
romance with Paris.

LATER IN LENINGRAD

There were no *troikas* that winter.
The Neva flowed and I had loved
no poets yet.
Instead I admired the preserved face of Lenin
as we were supposed to.
And there was St. Basil's
– icons, gold and beauty.
In a hairdressers, we sipped coffee and bought
roubles with US dollars.

There was Olga, tall and in love with our
Canadian friend.
For two nights she loved him
and I studied how she grasped him.
In tea-rooms by the Arbat,
I was mistaken for an English girl
by soldiers who sang opera and tried
to make me smile.
And later in Leningrad
– I stood still.

I stood still
and I remembered its first name.

LAZARUS LOVE

It's your photographs I prefer.
You seem better there,
like a ghost I'm still not afraid of.

And now you are old
and love is a discovered
artefact – petrified stone
of the kind you labelled in boxes.

A geological reason to believe
it all existed once,
while your ghost crept inside
images of you – slight resurrections
of how you could have been.

And now you are
half-stranger/half-father,
sipping coffee with me
as we discuss memories that would suit
this new Lazarus Love.

LADY MACBETH

Oh Lady,
you are full of death
and consigned to hell.
Love has torn you down
and your Lord has turned his face.
The night is waiting black
and the blood, red on your
hands, will not wash.

CLAUDEL

When your brain ceased to
skew madly,
at him
at his adoring lovers
at all lies.
When he no longer held your
foot in his palm,
then your fingers fed stone
with all the blazing of your heart.
Claudel,
tell me.
Is madness worth it?

GOODBYE

It is day.
You are leaving.
Over coffee we bid
goodbye to the lives
we've loved.
To our mad nights
and the precious fears
we've treasured.
Inevitable.
But I am human enough
to pray that your dreams
are braided with echoes of me.

SWAN

From the edge of a forest lake
swans glided
– white beads on grey glass.
It was October and the rain had stopped.
Hunters stood on the hill.
A girl stood at a half-open window
and watched the swans' necks loop into the air.
The hunters fell back until they were
no more than ants,
and the swans' beaks unzipped
the lake and dipped for fish.

The girl touched the clean, cold
glass; turning her thumb
like a swan's neck
feeling the tongue of cold
like water inside her.

I Saw Beckett the Other Day

I saw Beckett the other day
in the doorway of that café
where you took his photograph.

You know the one
... when he looked up at the lens
and realised how he could
haunt us all.

'Hey Beckett', I said
rejoicing in my discovery of him;
his hand on the door, his eyes
skimming over the interior image
of cigarette smoke and coffee.

I stood beside him. He rubbed his face so
he might recognise me. I smiled and
said even I didn't know what was
happening these days.
Even I could not stop the end.

He nodded, coughed and looked sly; his teeth were
yellow over the pink rim of his lips.
He mentioned the photograph. He said his face
had collected worms under the skin as if ready for
death and he smiled to show them dance
spasmatic with age-spots and veins.

Someone entered the café. Someone left.
Beckett touched the hair above my ear.
I stood on tip-toe so he could whisper down.

He said nothing. It was just a kiss
with the cold wind at our feet and the
smoke and egg friendly air
released in draughts between
the opening and closing of the café door;

which he stepped through to find his table
and entered some other world,
under greasy lights
coupled with table shine and coffee cups,
and thoughts of death, where she stood
groomed for an entrance, were held back by
the odd moments of life
that still strung the useful breaths
Beckett used to blow his coffee cool.

CRICKETS

after Andrew Wyeth's *Christina's World*

He gave me a dress
to cover my knees
and the lace on the hem
whispers on my skin.

He works in the cornfields.
He works in the house.
The window is a frame for his face.
I lie on the ground
where crickets like to find me.
I used to snap off their legs
and he helped me.

Now we live – with our own
world inside us
and between us
foreign to the 'hellos' of others.

The yellow grass bites.
The crickets are alive.
If I lift my dress, they walk
on my skin
like his fingers.

LICK

There is a lick of heaven
in my head.
A small slice of brain
lifted from its anchor.
It gives me dreams
and it keeps something fed.
As if my soul exists
like a worm
digesting horror,
smoothing it into
thought
then into words
listed, blasted
moulded, welded.

From a human voice it comes.
Like a crawling thing it comes.
Like something from
clay and given life it comes.

It hitches its limbs to me
and calls out
for love.

I'VE DISCARDED MY OLD SKIN

I've discarded my old skin
at the sea
with other split-open shells,
purple dead mussels
and slivers of fish bone.
My hips will fit different hands.
I am simple again.
Born with extra spit and
finally useless to you.

I Do Not Know How To

I do not know how to (do) die,
It comes to me in *blanks*
between words which hang
like abandoned limbs after the
soul has skipped off and left her
underskirts in my mind.

I do not know how to live sometimes
a measly recipe to fill one day and
another yet I discover words like jewels
and pack my stomach full against
the painted grin of death in my own reflection.

I do not know how to (do) die.
And that is a repeat.
A concertina of pressed down love,
squeaked clean and sweet.
So I fit my fear into the jigsaw
of my face
like anyone else but

I do not know how to live at times
Like any other ghost
caught in someone else's smile.

I LOST THE PLOT SOMEWHERE

I lost the plot somewhere
so I went looking at night
and negative men were in the trees
with their hang-dog mouths
and promises of extinction.
It's easy to believe them.
It's easy to see their sex
as something that might kill.
But I've found a way round
and it is just a little thing
but it is how the hot air
settles on my shoulders,
drops of sweat,
and the night has facets of
light, where jungle vines
whip and breathe down into
the earth beneath my feet.

I think of scorpions, spiders
and the deep growls above,
the thick movement of muscle
reaching into me
where words come,
with their raw skin
covering as the earth is
covered, concealing yet
turning its belly so that
my hand can fit in,
feeling a heart's bulbous
pump, feeling it register
in me, in the hot seethe of
the trees,
where the negative men
sweat and dig for me.

BETRAYAL

You slammed love away into
the cold quarters of your heart.
It creaked.
You poured bile to deaden it.
I saw all this.
I lamented without your permission.
You were loved.
You were betrayed.
You maintain that true betrayal
comes from a lover.
Ignorant lie.
We all strip our souls for any kind
of love and anyone can betray
with panache.

Van Gogh Visits

Van Gogh visits
my blue and yellow room.
At first, he looks like his
shifting portrayals
then he smiles like his self-portraits could.
He draws the crows in the air.
He sits cross-legged from me,
admiring my blue and yellow depths.
Sunflowers beam at us, dancing in my cheap poster.

I tell him I hear the crows caw.
He shrugs.
I write about his face and he watches.
He will not paint for me.
Not even for my walls.
He moves about on strong feet.
His clothes smell of sweat.
He likes what my pen paints.
He knows I want his passion.

TAKE IT FROM THE SPLEEN, BABY DOLL

Take it from the spleen, Baby Doll,
The heart ain't no good
for hate or love.
It digs a hole it can't get out
and nothing grows
with all the misery it wants to
solve.
Take it from the spleen, Little Girl,
with your Emily Dickinson flair;
maybe find a man
and sit on a rose garland chair
or some bed
made erotic
yet sweet
– as if your innocence unwrapped
is all the food you need to eat.
Take it from the spleen – you tell him,
little sister,
the heart just pumps it steady.
While the spleen
– oh my the spleen
oh my the spleen
— it gets you ready.

I was banned from my Great Aunt's House in New York.
My Great Aunt had jewels on her fingers.
She spoke to Mafia men on a daily basis,
and I danced barefoot on a table somewhere
while a ne'er do well lit matches to
shine up my toes.

I was banned from my Great Aunt's House in New York
because it wasn't the done thing
to love a man with a mole on his chin,
who danced me into dark corners
and had *no obvious career prospects*.

Except that sometimes he and I
listened to things that weren't exactly
tactile,
didn't have pulp
until we put it there
in words and pictures.
And my Great Aunt in New York
with her done ways,
had God in mind when she prayed

while we had the world
and its soft guts in our hearts.

EXPERIENCES OF A MAN IN GREAT DEBT TO ESTHER

She steps out of the Old Testament.
She sits opposite me and drinks vodka
from the glass I present her with.
She is thirsty, she says. Thirsty for
something other than a weak king and the demands
of a people she has prostituted herself for.
I cough and suggest that she is wrong.
Her eyes are two slivers of hard light above
the rim of her glass. She presses her tongue against it
and remarks at how lonely she is. She says she is
weary of the games she has played with her king and
confesses that she forgets his name at numerous points of
the day.

Morning ... while her dreams are dying but she still has
their taste in her mouth, and when a child screams in
pain, Esther fits into that pain; feels it shave joy from her
womb. She is still alive then ... and later ... when she has
washed his semen from her, she leans against a darkened
wall and dreams that her freedom can be moments like
these; free of him, free from surrender; absolved from the
murders of Haman's children ... and the bloody ties to
Uncle Mordechai.

I wait until her silence makes me speak. My pills are round
white little eyes on that table beside me. Headaches are
necessary now, I explain. They keep my breath going.
I laugh to sound normal. It is night and I am having
another madness, yet Esther's dress captivates me.
It comes from a 1930s film. A skin of silk for her body. It
catches the light as she moves. As do her teeth and the
jewels tied in her hair.

I am having a dream, she says. We drink more vodka and I
resolve not to take the pills just yet, although they twist

and wink in the shadows. I tell her that I had read her story in a classroom years ago. I tell her I thought it was love that made the king reach out his sceptre to her. *And he realised the error of his ways*, I remind her. *He killed for you. Isn't that a triumph?* Esther begins to cry. I watch how her lips catch tears for her tongue. I open the book to her story and try to see the same woman there. But she does not appear. *You don't exist*, I tell her. She shakes her head and reaches for the necklace around her neck. *He put it there*, she says. *He says they are for love. And the people kiss my feet as I pass. I exist too much.* Then she smiles at me.

Am I the best to come to you?
Yes, I say. I always say the same no matter who asks.
Judith, she wonders, but I shake my head.
Esther thinks for a minute: *Jezebel?*
Hardly ever, I maintain. *She's too ambitious. Expects too much. Eve?*
She resents what happened, I reply. *She doesn't like me.*
And me, Esther asks. *What about me?*
So I think of her king and his weak love, slithering from her to Haman. I think of that love like the burst insides of a serpent, gluing into a shape, seeking a skin that could be worshipped by his queen, and so create him as a man.

I take one pill to soothe the edges of my brain.
Esther sips her vodka. She says that she likes my room.
I take another pill. She leans close so that her breath hums on my lips and sets fire to my tongue.
She kisses the pill away and inside me ... in that place where things are born, life begins like the shifting skin on her body. Esther smiles. She is in no hurry. Her husband may have found a concubine to replace her. She asks if I have any snakes. I shake my head. I am writing. The madness dims to two twin points in my brain.
Tweedle Dum and Tweedle Dee, Esther lisps.

She is looking for snakes and walks around my room.
Her skin whispers against the walls. She mewls for reptiles
and one switches Its tail across my feet then dips between
my toes. Its tongue is dark red, twin tails of glistening felt.
Esther leans on my shoulders and follows my sentences
with her long fingers while the snake trails upwards, using
its fangs to open her. She shudders in my ears like the soft
roll of sex between us. I could catch her yet I cannot.
Like Cleopatra, she whispers and the snake settles inside
her breast. Esther returns to her chair.
I write on as she dissolves.

Later I wake into a cold room with the radio bleating,
My pills minus two in a small circle beside the vodka.
I do not look at my words just yet. I make coffee and go
outside. The morning is wet and new and I feel as I always
do ... at the end of such nights ... created in skin and bone
... created as man.

ABOUT THE AUTHOR

Órfhlaith Foyle was born in Nigeria to Irish parents and has lived in Africa and Australia. She is currently based in Galway. Her first novel, the critically-acclaimed *Belios*, was published in 2005 by The Lilliput Press. A collection of her short fiction and poetry, *Revenge*, was published in 2005 by Arlen House and is available internationally from Syracuse University Press. She is currently working on her second novel.

ACKNOWLEDGEMENTS

Thanks to the editors of the following publications where some of these poems first appeared: *Succour, The SHOp, The Stinging Fly* and *Ulster Tatler: Literary Miscellany*. The poems *Romance with Paris* and *Crickets* were first published in *Postcard Poems*, a collaboratory poetry project with Nuala Ní Chonchúir in 2009.

My thanks go to Nuala Ní Chonchúir, fellow poet, collaborator and dear friend for all her advice, encouragement and stalwart support.